IMAGES
of England

MINING IN CORNWALL
VOLUME FOUR:
HAYLE TO KERRIER & CARRICK

IMAGES
of England

MINING IN CORNWALL
VOLUME FOUR:
HAYLE TO KERRIER & CARRICK

Compiled by
L.J. Bullen

For my wife, Margaret

TEMPUS

Other Tempus Titles Include:

Mining In Cornwall Volume One: The Central District.
J.H. Trounson & L.J. Bullen.   £9.99
0 7524 1707 X.

Mining In Cornwall Volume Two: The County Explored.
J.H. Trounson & L.J. Bullen.   £9.99
0 7524 1708 8.

Mining In Cornwall Volume Three: Penwith and South Kerrier.
L.J. Bullen.   £9.99
0 7524 1759 2.

The Early British Tin Industry.
Sandy Gerrard.   £14.99
0 7524 1452 6.

Stone Quarry Landscapes.
Peter Stainer.   £16.99
0 7524 1451 7.

First published in 2001 by Tempus Publishing
Reprinted 2004

Reprinted in 2010 by
The History Press
The Mill, Brimscombe Port,
Stroud, Gloucestershire, GL5 2QG
www.thehistorypress.co.uk

Reprinted in 2011

© L.J. Bullen, 2011

The right of L.J. Bullen to be identified as the Author
of this work has been asserted in accordance with the
Copyrights, Designs and Patents Act 1988.

All rights reserved. No part of this book may be reprinted
or reproduced or utilised in any form or by any electronic,
mechanical or other means, now known or hereafter invented,
including photocopying and recording, or in any information
storage or retrieval system, without the permission in writing
from the Publishers.

British Library Cataloguing in Publication Data.
A catalogue record for this book is available from the British Library.

ISBN 978 0 7524 2133 9

Typesetting and origination by Tempus Publishing.
Printed and bound in England.

Contents

Acknowledgements 6

Introduction 7

1. Around St Hilary, Breage, Hayle and Gwinear 9

2. Wendron to Falmouth 27

3. Feock to Gwennap and Camborne-Redruth 49

4. Chacewater to the Atlantic Coast 103

Acknowledgements

A number of persons have rendered assistance to me in connection with the production of this book. I should like to record my grateful thanks for all their help:

John Burn, Brian Errington, Peter Gilson of the Royal Cornwall Polytechnic Society,

Glen Jones, Keith Pope, Eric Rabjohns and, in particular, my daughter Anne Smith together with my son-in-law Robert Smith.

I also wish to thank my publishers for their continued encouragement and support.

Introduction

This volume contains around two hundred images drawn from a very large number of prints covering the localities indicated in the title. In general it includes some of the smaller mines from the South coast to the North coast in Kerrier and Carrick. Once again space restrictions have meant that much interesting material has to await publication at a later date.

The world confers upon Cornwall the accolade 'The home of hard-rock mining and the cradle of the steam engine.' It is hoped that, in some small way, this series of volumes will help the professional and amateur student more easily understand the great industry that once existed in the Duchy.

L.J. Bullen, Camborne, Cornwall, January 2001

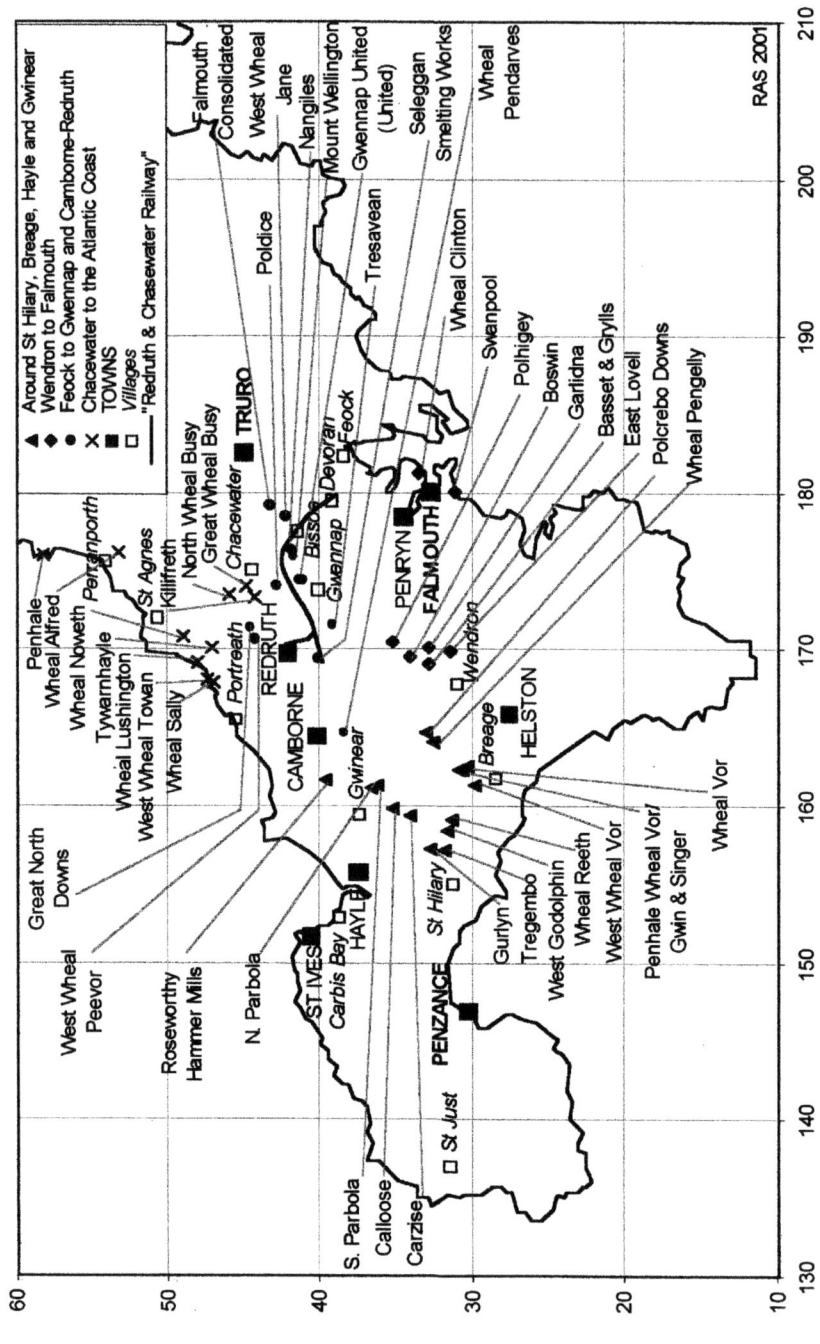

A guide to Mine locations appearing in the text. Axes show British National Grid References.

One
Around St Hilary, Breage, Hayle and Gwinear

Wheal Reeth / Lady Gwendolen. An early photograph of the last re-working of the mine in about 1930. This shows the headgear and trestle to the waste dump. The terminal pole of the electricity supply line can be seen on the left. All of the plant was electrically powered.

Wheal Reeth / Lady Gwendolen, c.1930. Another photograph taken during the same period of re-working. A group of employees is assembled under the trestle.

Wheal Reeth / Lady Gwendolen, c.1913. Two steam engines, which provided power for the small treatment plant.

Wheal Reeth / Lady Gwendolen. A display of wooden pumps and chain & hook handle of a rag and chain pump. These relics were found underground at the twenty-fathom level below adit in 1929.

Wheal Reeth. The headgear on an adit shaft in the 1920s/30s re-working.

Gurlyn Mine, near Relubbus. A view of the operations in the early twentieth-century re-working.

North Parbola Mine. Prospecting plant erected in the early 1920s.

North Parbola Mine. Another view of the plant erected in the 1920s.

North Parbola Mine. A group of workers and visitors to the mine during the re-working, which took place in the early twentieth century.

North Parbola Mine, which is situated just south of the hamlet of Wall near Gwinear. A general view of the early twentieth-century re-working at Medlyn's Shaft, which was locally known as Incline shaft. The operations were short-lived.

North Parbola Mine, c.1906. Medlyn's Shaft, showing the headgear and skip road. A steam winch with a vertical boiler is in the partially clad building. The small mill building is in the background.

North Parbola Mine, c.1906. A general view of the re-opening of the mine.

South Parbola Mine, c.1906. A view of the early twentieth-century re-working. This shows the original Cornish pumping engine house being used as an ore bin. Just to the left of the stack can be seen a grinding pan for the fine crushing of the tin ore. In the background is the fitting shop / carpenters shop. The tall headgear is unusual in that it has no boom stays. In the foreground left is the electricity generating room which provided power for the pumps. On the right is the steam winding engine house.
Photograph: S.J. Govier.

South Parbola Mine, c.1906. This internal view of the generating room shows the gas engines which drove the dynamos being erected.

South Parbola Mine, c.1909. A later view showing the mill building behind the engine house. The group of miners using a windlass in the foreground appear to be re-collaring an old shaft. Photograph courtesy of Mr G. Jones.

Harvey & Co., Hayle. The erecting shop of this famous firm of engineers in 1876. Here can be seen a Bull Engine with a 22in cylinder and 6ft stroke, which was supplied to the Kimberley Diamond Mines in South Africa.

Harvey & Co., Hayle. As with nearly all engineering in Cornwall the famous foundries owed their origins to the Mining Industry. They eventually supplied machinery to mining fields worldwide. The government of Holland commissioned three large pumping engines from Cornish foundries to dewater Haarlem Lake in the 1840s. These were to have massive cylinders of 144in diameter. This photograph shows the first (miscast) cylinder for the Cruquis engine. This was later used as a moulding pit for other large cylinders produced in the foundry.

The Roseworthy Hammer Mills, c.1900. In the foreground is the holding pond and sluice, which was the source of water to drive the wheels providing power to the tilt hammers and other machinery. The Tuckingmill Foundry Co. at Camborne operated this site until 1910 and the last owners were J. & F. Pool of Hayle.

Roseworthy Hammer Mills, c.1900. An internal view showing the guillotine being used in the manufacture of Cornish shovels, a pile of which (with no hilts) are on the floor by the foot of the operator.

Calloose Mine, Gwinear. This was a part of Trevaskis Mine, which commenced operations under the name of "Calloose Mines". It was an under capitalised and doubtful flotation, which commenced about 1919. No production ensued. The scene shows the partially completed mill building.

Carzise Mine, near Leedstown. The mill building and new stack, c.1926. This was another scheme that failed, by the same promoters who were involved with the Calloose Mine.

Wheal Pengelly, Nancegollan. The house contained a 36in pumping engine. The mine was very dry and the engine only made a stroke every four minutes or so. On one occasion an engine driver was reprimanded for being late on shift. His excuse was that as he was walking over the downs on his way to work he stopped to watch the engine make a stroke, thus causing his late arrival!
Photograph: Eric Rabjohns.

Polcrebo Downs Mine, near Nancegollan. The engine house and truncated stack on the Engine Shaft in the 1930s. The mine had ceased work in 1890.

West Godolphin Mine (known locally as "Wheal Junket"), formerly North Greatwork Mine. This house on Pressure Shaft once contained a 60in pumping engine. The photograph was taken about sixty years after the mine closed in 1890.

Tregembo Mine, Relubbus. A photograph taken in the 1980s of the pumping engine house on this mine, which once contained a 60in engine.

Penhale Wheal Vor and Gwin & Singer, c.1890. On the left are Hollingsworth's 60in engine and Holroyd's 40in engine of Penhale Wheal Vor, which had then recently closed. On the right of the scene are the stamps engine, headgear, capstan shears, pumping engine house, waste dump and winding engine house on Ann's shaft of Gwin & Singer Mine, which is at work.

West Wheal Vor. The derelict mill buildings in the 1920s. Attempts to re-open Carleen Mine as West Wheal Vor in the early years of the twentieth century were not successful due to pumping problems.

Wheal Vor, May 1906. The proposal to re-open the mine caused much enthusiasm with the promise of employment, trade etc. The view of timber being delivered seems to have attracted many local inhabitants.

Wheal Vor, 1906. Crease's Shaft shortly before work commenced on re-constructing the shaft collar.

Wheal Vor. Crease's Shaft, showing the erection of the steam winding engine in the 1906 reopening. This attempt to re-work the mine ended in failure. However the winding engine was purchased by the Geevor Mine at Pendeen. Here it served for over thirty years before being replaced by an electric hoist.

Wheal Vor, 1906. Early operations in the re-opening of the mine. Two Lancashire boilers have been delivered.

Wheal Vor, c.1908. Crease's Shaft (also known as Borlase's Shaft). All the plant is fully operational and the un-watering of the mine is in progress.

Wheal Vor. A further view of Crease's Shaft at the time of the early twentieth-century attempted re-opening.

Two
Wendron to Falmouth

Polhigey Mine, Wendron, 1926. The wooden headgear is being erected on the first shaft, which was known as No.1 Shaft.

Polhigey Mine, Wendron. Early operations in 1926, when the first shaft of the mine was being sunk. Various ancillary buildings and tramroads are in evidence. To the left are new dwelling houses, which were built by the company for their employees.

Polhigey Mine, 1926. The building to house the winding engine on No.1 Shaft is under construction.

Polhigey Mine, *c*.1927. No.1 Shaft complex is complete, fully operational and shaft sinking is in progress.

Polhigey Mine, Roberts Shaft, *c*.1926, showing the sinking headgear and hoist when the shaft was commenced.

Polhigey Mine, Roberts Shaft, c.1926. On the left is the electricity generating station under construction. On the right is the sinking headgear on Roberts Shaft.

Polhigey Mine, Roberts Shaft, c.1926. The permanent steel headgear is near completion and the electricity generating station is in an advanced state of construction. In the background is the headgear on No.1 Shaft.

Polhigey Mine, c.1927. The mill site showing the aerial ropeway connecting it with Roberts Shaft which was a considerable distance away. The last Brunton Arsenic Calciner to be erected in Cornwall is visible at the left of the ropeway terminal with the flue leading to the stack. The overhead electricity line bringing power from the Generating Station at Roberts Shaft is on the left.

Polhigey Mine, c.1927. On the skyline left of centre is Roberts Shaft and the conveyor to the ore bin feeding the aerial ropeway. On the right the headgear and long dump at No.1 Shaft are visible. This photograph was taken near the mill site.

Polhigey Mine, c.1927. The mill site viewed from Medlyn Moor. On the left skyline the headgear and ore bin at Roberts Shaft are just discernible.

Polhigey Mine, c.1927. A further view of the mill. The Nissen stamps are on the right and the dressing tables and other mill plant in the building on the left. In the framework on the right is the tension pulley of the ropeway.

Polhigey Mine, c.1927. Roberts Shaft showing the electric winder house, headgear, landing brace, crusher station and conveyor carrying the crushed ore to the aerial ropeway bin. The large building in the background is the electricity generating station, which contained diesel engines providing the power for generation and an air compressor.

Polhigey Mine, c.1927. Roberts Shaft. A similar view to the previous photograph but showing the ore bin and ropeway terminal. Here the buckets were loaded for their journey to the mill. Note the waterproof canvas suspended on the ore bin to protect the men loading the buckets.

Polhigey Mine, c.1927. The complex around Roberts Shaft showing the headgear, ore bin, ropeway terminal and first ropeway tower. In the background is the Power Station building and the terminal pole of the overhead electricity line serving the mill and No.1 Shaft.

Polhigey Mine, c.1930. Roberts Shaft. The headgear has been felled and is being cut up for scrap. Note the men with sledgehammers and the oxygen and acetylene cylinders on and by the lorry. When the mine closed S.J. Andrew & Son of Redruth bought the plant. The stamps and some other mill equipment were sold to the Mount Wellington Mine.

Boswin Mine, known locally as "The Puffet". Early operations around Main Shaft, c.1907. The headgear is being erected and a tramway to the dump is being laid. The shaft was eventually deepened to sixty fathoms.

Boswin Mine. A later photograph taken in about 1912 showing the mill when the mine was in production. The mine was opened by two former Camborne School of Mines students.

Boswin Mine, Main Shaft, c.1911. Taken when the mine was in full operation. Left to right: headgear on Main Shaft and trestle to the mill.

Boswin Mine, Main Shaft. The scene in the 1920s when the mine had been long abandoned.

Basset & Grylls Mine (also known at various times as Porkellis Mine and Jantar Mine). A view of the first mill erected in the early twentieth-century re-working.

Basset & Grylls Mine. Old Mens Shaft headgear and steam winding engine house. Taken in the early 1920s when the mine had temporarily closed down because of the low price of tin. It was on care and maintenance and eventually re-opened.

Basset & Grylls Mine. Old Mens Shaft around 1926 showing the double track tramway which connected the shaft to the mill. The waggons were propelled by attaching a clip to the endless wire rope, taking full cars in one direction and returning empties in the other.

Basset & Grylls Mine. Old Mens Shaft. A general view in the mid-1920s.

Basset & Grylls Mine, c.1930. Old Mens Shaft. Another view from the south-west. By this time the steam winding engine had been replaced by an electric hoist.

Basset & Grylls Mine, Old Mens Shaft. A view of the compact arrangement taken from the road in the early 1930s.

Basset & Grylls Mine. An early 1900s view of the milling plant showing the small burning house with an iron chimney stack.

Basset & Grylls Mine, Old Mens Shaft. A 1920s view from the entrance gates showing exhaust steam from the engine, which drove the pitwork for the pumps.

Basset & Grylls Mine, Spring 1920. Old Mens Shaft at the time a new Holman built steam winder was being installed. A new steel stack is about to be hoisted.

Basset & Grylls Mine, Spring 1920. Old Mens Shaft. The new stack is in the process of being hauled into place on the concrete base.

Basset & Grylls Mine, Old Mens Shaft, April 1920. The new stack is in place and the guy ropes fitted.

East Lovell Mine, Colonel's Shaft, c.1927. A prospecting headgear and small steam hoist erected during the work carried out by the Anglo Oriental Corporation.

Garlidna Mine, New Shaft (part of North Lovell Mine), c.1913. A small headgear and steam hoist erected during an attempted re-working between 1912 and 1916.

Garlidna Mine, c.1914. The small mill erected at the time of the partial re-opening of the mine.

43

Garlidna Mine, c.1914. Another view of the mill.

Wheal Clinton, Flushing. A lead mine reputed to have been at work between 1854 and 1859. This print dates from the late 1860s.

Swanpool Mine, Falmouth, from a painting by J. Knight in 1856. This was a lead mine which had been worked from the mid-eighteenth century until 1860, albeit with periods of being idle.

Swanpool Mine, Falmouth, c.1880. The chimney stack built on Pennance Point (Stack Point) to disperse fumes from the lead smelting works of the mine. Much later an arsenic refinery was built on the site of the smelter which utilised the same stack.

Swanpool Mine, Falmouth, 1920s. A view from the cliff footpath to Gyllyngvase beach at Falmouth and showing part of Swanpool beach in the foreground. On the left is the mine count house and what at that time remained of the mine dump.

Swanpool Mine, Falmouth. The count house in 1920, by then in use as a dwelling, on a cold winter's day, to judge by the smoking chimneys. One wonders if the boy and girl have been searching the dump on the left and are examining a mineral specimen!

Swanpool Mine, early twentieth century. A view of the stack from the beach at Swanpool.

Three
Feock to Gwennap and Camborne – Redruth

Bissoe, c.1900. One of the many Tinstreams and other works which gave much employment in the Carnon Valley. The large tubs, known as kieves, in which the Tin concentrate was stirred to upgrade it still further, are much in evidence. Two men in the background are carrying a handbarrow.

The Redruth & Chasewater Railway, c.1899. This 4ft gauge railway was built by John Taylor and Sons to serve their mining interests. It ran from tidewater at Devoran to the Basset Mines, which are south of the prominent landmark of Carn Brea between Camborne and Redruth. Near the summit of Lanner Hill there was a junction where the branch for Redruth commenced. This terminated by Pednandrea Mine, which is situated virtually in the town. In over nine miles it rose nearly 600ft from sea level. Commenced in 1824, it operated until 1915. Horses were employed until 1854 when locomotives were introduced. This scene shows the line where the long weighbridge loop commenced west of the crossing of the Truro-Falmouth road near Devoran. In the background left is the Brunel type viaduct, which carried the branch line of the Great Western Railway from Truro to Falmouth. Photograph courtesy of John Burn who now lives in "The Poplars".

Redruth & Chasewater Railway, *c.*1900. Locomotive Miner and twelve-waggon coal train in the Carnon valley.

Redruth & Chasewater Railway, *c.*1899. The Ting Tang watering place above the village of Carharrack. The driver standing by the locomotive was named Brewer and the guard was called Tom Lavin. The fireman is by the water tank on the left.

Redruth & Chasewater Railway, c.1899. Locomotive *Miner* carrying out shunting operations. Left to right: The fireman, driver Brewer and the guard Tom Lavin.

Redruth & Chasewater Railway, c.1899. A train on Buller Downs, near the uppermost terminus of the line. In addition to serving the John Taylor-controlled mines, the railway carried supplies for other mines and private businesses along its route between Devoran, Redruth and the Basset Mines. In its busiest times as much as 100,000 tons was carried by the line annually.

Redruth & Chasewater Railway, c.1900. Locomotive *Miner* and train approaching Great Yard near Carharrack. In the heyday of the railway, Great Yard was a major junction with long horse-worked branches serving the United Mines and the Consolidated Mines.

West Wheal Jane, Beecher's Shaft, c.1908. When this mine was re-opened as part of the Falmouth Consolidated Mines Ltd. in 1905, Beecher's Shaft was one of a number which were refurbished. The scene shows a house containing a small steam winder, headgear, ore bin and horse-worked tramway, which conveyed the ore to the mill. The following two photos show Beecher's at subsequent re-openings.

West Wheal Jane, Beecher's Shaft, c.1940. When the mine was taken over by the Mount Wellington company in 1939 this shaft was again brought back into use. At this time electricity was utilised for pumping and a steam winch for hoisting.

West Wheal Jane, Beecher's Shaft, c.1970. In the late 1960s the mine was re-opened by Consolidated Goldfields Ltd who named it Wheal Jane. This will undoubtedly confuse all future mining historians as there was already a Wheal Jane dating back to 1740! The view shows the steel headgear prior to the electric hoist being installed.

Falmouth Consolidated Mines Ltd, c.1911. In 1905 a company was formed under this title, to work: Sperries Mine, Wheal Hope & Falmouth Mine, West Jane Mine, West Wheal Jane, Wheal Widden and Nangiles Mine. In the event, most operations were confined to Wheal Jane and West Wheal Jane. This scene shows an internal view of the mill and in particular the Elmore Flotation Plant for the recovery of fine tin.

Falmouth Consolidated Mines Ltd, c.1907, showing the wooden headgear and hoist house on Falmouth Shaft. The arrangement at the shaft collar seems to indicate that bailing skips are in use in order to lower the water

Falmouth Consolidated Mines Ltd, c.1910. Green's Shaft headgear and ore bins.

Falmouth Consolidated Mines Ltd, Tremayne's Shaft, *c.*1908. This photograph should be compared with the photograph on page 71 of Volume 2 in this series. In this view we have an earlier scene with the original ore bin and headgear. At a later date the headgear was heightened and the ore bin enlarged.

Falmouth Consolidated Mines Ltd, *c.*1906. Giles Shaft in the early stages of the 1905-15 re-working. The steam plant was later replaced by an electric hoist when the generating station became operational.

Falmouth Consolidated Mines Ltd, c.1911. An internal view of the mill which contained sixty head of Californian stamps.

West Wheal Jane, Clemow's Shaft, c.1970. A second-hand former colliery headgear was purchased and is being erected on the shaft.

West Wheal Jane, No.2 Shaft, 1970. At this time it was decided to sink a new shaft in order to facilitate a more economic method of mining. The new shaft collar is on the left and the framework of the electric winder house is on the right.

West Wheal Jane, c.1970. Left to right: No.2 Shaft when being sunk with a single sheave wheel in the headgear; Baldhu church spire, and Clemow's Shaft with its early ex-colliery headgear.

West Wheal Jane, c.1970. No. 2 Shaft is on the left, Clemow's Shaft in the centre and the framework of the crusher station building is on the right.

West Wheal Jane, c.1972. A later photograph taken from approximately the same position as the previous one. Left to right: No.2 Shaft, which was used for men and materials; the complex of buildings such as winder houses, compressor house etc., and the new taller headgear on Clemow's Shaft now in use for ore hoisting; the conveyor to the crusher station and from the crusher station the conveyor to the ore stockpile. From this point a further conveyor carried the ore to the mill.

Carnon Consolidated Tin Mines Ltd prospecting plant, which was erected at Sampson's Shaft of the Gwennap United Mines in 1982. This portable equipment was designed for use throughout the considerable areas held under lease by the company.

Carnon Consolidated Tin Mines Ltd. In 1983 Cornish tin production was providing two-thirds of the annual requirement of the U.K. for that metal. In the same year the operating company of West Wheal Jane and Mount Wellington (C.C.T.M.L.) decided to sink a decline in the extreme west of the lease areas. This photograph shows miners at work in the 1 in 7 drift in 1984.

Carnon Consolidated Tin Mines Ltd, 1984. The portal of the decline in the Wheal Maid valley showing a scoop tram at the surface.

Mount Wellington Mine (also known as Wheal Magpie), c.1937. Taken at the time the mill was being erected. These were Nissen Stamps, which had previously worked at the Polhigey Mine. The dismantling and re-erection of this mill was undertaken by Langford Mining & Civil Engineering Contractors of Lanner, Redruth.

Mount Wellington Mine, late 1930s. A general view taken from the road showing the mill on the left with Robinson's Shaft winder and headgear on the right. From 1923 the principal workings of the mine were in a part of the Wheal Andrew section of the famous United Mines. After about seven years two companies were formed, between 1930 and 1935, which commenced developing the mine. By 1941 operations had ceased.

Mount Wellington Mine. In the 1960s a Canadian based company under the title 'Cornwall Tin & Mining Corporation' commenced a diamond drilling programme and eventually sank a new 15ft diameter shaft, which was named Amy Shaft. This was only a short distance from the old Robinson's Shaft. A considerable amount of work was carried out in refurbishing the adit of the mine. This early 1970s view shows the old adit excavated as a cutting into which was laid a large diameter concrete pipe to form a new adit. On the skyline are the foundations of the Nissen Stamps from the previous working in the 1930s and 1940s.

Mount Wellington Mine, early 1970s, showing the work involved in re-making the adit. Concrete is being poured over the pipe, which formed the new adit course. The old adit leading to the new Amy shaft is seen on the left.

Mount Wellington Mine, Amy Shaft, early 1970s. The sinking headgear is complete and the commencement of shaft sinking will shortly be taken in hand. In the background is the Engine Shaft of Nangiles Mine with a wooden prospecting headgear, which Consolidated Goldfields had erected prior to the re-opening of Wheal Jane.

Mount Wellington Mine, Amy Shaft, early 1970s. The erection of the permanent winding engine and house after shaft sinking was completed.

Mount Wellington Mine, Amy Shaft, early 1970s. On the left the mill complex is being built. The headgear is in the process of reconstruction, making it higher to accommodate the ore handling facilities.

Mount Wellington Mine, 1970s. The new mill during construction.

Mount Wellington Mine, Amy Shaft, early 1970s. Work is in progress on the building of the ore bins near the shaft collar.

Mount Wellington Mine, 1975. A view from the northern side of the valley showing the complex around Amy Shaft when the mine was in production. The offices and workshops are on the left of the headgear with the mill on the right.
Photograph K.M. Trathen ARPS.

Mount Wellington Mine, 1975. Taken from the hillside to the south of the site with the mill building on the left and Amy Shaft, offices and workshops on the right. In the background left is the mill of Wheal Jane.
Photograph K.M. Trathen ARPS.

Nangiles Mine, Engine Shaft, 1960s. In the late 1960s Consolidated Goldfields were examining this area with a view to re-opening West Jane Mine. They refurbished this shaft and erected a wooden headgear, which had first been in use at the Cligga Mine, Perranporth. A small electric hoist was also installed. The derelict engine house had contained an 80in Cornish pumping engine in the nineteenth century. In the right background is the engine house and stack at Shears shaft, in the Cusvey section of the famous nineteenth century Consolidated Mines.

Nangiles Mine, Engine Shaft, 1967. It will be noted that the headgear boom stays have a frame and pulleys fitted. This was to enable the double drum electric winder to haul direct to a single large cage and have a counterpoise, with the rope off set by the pulley wheels in the frame. The old engine house eventually had to be almost entirely demolished for safety reasons.

United Mines, early twentieth century. A headgear erected by two Camborne School of Mines graduates who, it is believed, were funded by their parents! It has not been possible to identify which shaft this spindly looking structure was erected at. It was never completed and the young mining engineers left to seek their fortune elsewhere in the world of mining.

Poldice Mine. Tin dressing plant set up by the Berrida (Nigeria) Tin Fields Ltd at Poldice in about 1918. This operation was entirely steam powered and had an extensive horse-worked tramway to bring dump material to the mill. A unique feature of the dressing floors was a set of round frames with decks made of corrugated glass. A novel experiment, which was a complete failure! The stamps and the steam engine that drove them were purchased by the Kingsdown Mining Co. for further use at St Austell.

Poldice Mine. The site of the dressing floors of this great mine has been host to three further dressing plants during the twentieth century. The Berrida Company was the first of these, followed by a company headed by the late Edgar Trestrail in the early 1920s. This photograph shows the latter operation, which consisted of a ten-head battery of Californian Stamps and a small dressing plant.

Poldice Mine, late 1920s. The mill under construction for the Park an Chy Mine was the third to be erected at Poldice in the twentieth century. The mine was some distance away and it was therefore decided to construct an aerial ropeway to convey the ore to a convenient mill site at Poldice.

Poldice Mine, late 1920s. A later view of the Park an Chy mine Mill at Poldice, showing the aerial ropeway bin, crusher station and stamps. In the background are the extensive dumps of Creegbrawse Mine, which is one of the oldest tin and copper mines in Cornwall.

Great North Downs Mine. This extensive mine dates from the latter part of the eighteenth century. After being idle for a great many years the area was chosen for a diamond drilling programme by Camborne Tin Ltd. This scene shows the drill rig at the commencement of the first hole to be drilled on Saturday 21st September 1963. In the period from the early 1960s to the time of the international tin price collapse of 1985 a great deal of mining exploratory work was carried out in the Duchy.

West Wheal Peevor. In the 1960s a South African Company, Barcas Mining Corporation, commenced operations preparatory to prospecting this mine. The scene shows the erection of the prospecting headgear on Mitchell's Shaft. It is interesting to note that in a previous working this was the first shaft in Cornwall to have a cage fitted i.e. the ore was raised in a waggon in a cage rather than being hauled in a skip.
Photo. Bob Matthews.

West Wheal Peevor, c.1967. In this view we see the house which originally contained a 50in Cornish pumping engine at Mitchell's Shaft. In the foreground a house for the electric winch is being constructed and the headgear is partly visible on the right.
Photo: Bob Matthews.

West Wheal Peevor, Mitchell's Shaft, c.1967. The electric winch and headgear are in place.
Photograph: Bob Matthews.

West Wheal Peevor, Mitchell's Shaft, c.1968. A slightly earlier view showing the old 50in Cornish pumping engine house and the headgear.
Photograph: Bob Matthews.

West Wheal Peevor, Mitchell's Shaft, c.1967. The plant as it appeared when pumping commenced. The figure on the right is Bob Matthews, who was supervising the work.

West Wheal Peevor, Mitchell's Shaft, c.1967. The electric winch that was used for the shaftwork. Photograph: Bob Matthews.

Tresavean Mine, Lanner, Harvey's Engine Shaft, c.1911. The mine was re-opened in 1910 and the former 90in pumping engine house was converted into an electricity generating station. This view shows the greatly heightened stack to provide sufficient draught for three high pressure Lancashire boilers. The boiler house framing is in the foreground and the headgear is being erected.

Tresavean Mine, Harvey's Engine Shaft, c.1910. The former engine house had an extension built at the side as there was insufficient room to house all the electricity generating sets. This was taken at the time the mine was being dewatered using electric pumps.

Tresavean Mine, c.1910. Harvey's Engine Shaft during the dewatering operations. It will be noted that on top of the headgear there is a single sheave wheel. This was used during the dewatering for a skip or man cage (which were interchangeable) plus a ladderway. The two main compartments in the shaft were used to take a sinking pump in each with all necessary cables as well as a temporary 6in rising main. The two sheave wheels for these are visible at a lower point in the headgear.

Tresavean Mine, Harvey's Engine Shaft, c.1910. A further view during the dewatering showing the boiler house and winder in the foreground. The former pumping engine house contained the electric generators. The headgear clearly shows the configuration of the sheave wheels as described in the last caption.

Tresavean Mine, c.1909. A view of the mill under construction.

Tresavean Mine, Harvey's Engine Shaft, c.1915. A general view from the north-west. The very large permanent steam winder is now in service and is housed in the building in the background. The Blacksmith's shop is on the right. A horse-drawn waggon is delivering pipes, which are being off-loaded under the tripod and then placed onto the narrow gauge tramway. The building on the left was the former Stamps Engine House, which had been refurbished as an electricity substation. By this time the mine had ceased generation of its own electricity and was taking a supply from the public mains which was now available.

Tresavean Mine, Harvey's Engine Shaft. An internal composite photograph of the permanent steam winding engine. This engine was one of the most powerful steam hoists to be installed in Cornwall. The photograph was taken just after the mine ceased production in 1928 and when the plant was for disposal.

Tresavean Mine, 1920s. A group of mill workers by what appears to be a round frame at the bottom end of the mill site.

Tresavean Mine, 1920s. Some of the workforce, principally carpenters, each holding a tool of their trade.

Tresavean Mine, c.1910. A group of miners at the shaft collar of Harvey's Engine Shaft. The massive bob wall of the old engine house forms the background to this scene at the time of the dewatering of the mine.

Tresavean Mine. Surface workers in the 1920s.

Tresavean Mine, c.1914. A general view of the mill and dressing floors. Production of tin commenced at this time and it will be noticed that some final building work is being carried out.

Tresavean Mine, Harvey's Engine Shaft, c.1916. The mine was now fully equipped and in production. It was taking a supply of electricity from the public mains and the boilers of the former generating station were now supplying steam to the winding engine in the house on the left. Other auxiliary plants were also steamed from these boilers.

Seleggan Smelting Works, Carnkie near Redruth, c.1900. A view from the top of one of the stacks. This was the last tin smelter to operate in Cornwall and thereafter all tin concentrate was shipped elsewhere in the U.K. for smelting. For many years this works obtained all its coal supplies via the Redruth & Chasewater Railway.

Seleggan Smelting Works, Carnkie near Redruth, c.1900. A further bird's-eye view of part of the extensive works.

Seleggan Smelting Works, Carnkie near Redruth, showing the construction of the last stack to be built at the works in the early 1920s. The plant finally closed in 1931.

Wheal Pendarves, near Camborne, Simms Shaft, February 1967. After a diamond drilling programme, a consortium of Union Corporation (U.K.) Ltd and Tehidy Minerals Ltd decided to proceed with the sinking of a new shaft on the former Pendarves Estate. This shows the site after the cementation of the shaft area had been completed. Shaft sinking was to commence shortly.

Wheal Pendarves, Simms Shaft, 1967. The central cementation pipe for the shaft is evident in the middle of the photograph.

Wheal Pendarves, Simms Shaft, 1967. The collar of the shaft during initial sinking using a crane. The surveyor standing by the safety rail is the author.

Wheal Pendarves, Simms Shaft. The shaft collar in 1967.

Wheal Pendarves, Simms Shaft, 1967. A view from the top of the headgear, showing the main winder house with the sinking stage winches in front.

Wheal Pendarves, Simms Shaft, c.1968. Taken on the sheave platform on top of the headgear and showing the main winder sheave wheels with a smaller capstan wheel in use during the shaft sinking.

Wheal Pendarves, Simms Shaft, 1968. Another view from the top of the headgear showing the settlement lagoons for water pumped from underground.

Wheal Pendarves, Simms Shaft, 1967, showing the headgear, permanent winder and house under construction.

Wheal Pendarves, Simms Shaft. A further view of the headgear, winder house and electric winder being erected in 1967.

Wheal Pendarves, Simms Shaft, 1967. On the left are the stage winches used in connection with the shaft sinking. The drums of the main winder can be seen within the steel framework of the house under construction at the rear.

Wheal Pendarves, Simms Shaft, 1967. A view from inside the permanent winder house during the time of erection, showing the rope drums and post brakes. The headgear and temporary sinking crane are in the background.

Wheal Pendarves, Simms Shaft. The cactus grab is suspended within the headgear. This is used to load the sinking kibble after blasting at the shaft bottom. The photograph was taken during the sinking of the shaft in the autumn of 1967.

Wheal Pendarves, Simms Shaft, 1968. A view looking down the shaft from the collar when only about fifty feet deep, showing the concrete lining.

Wheal Pendarves, Simms Shaft, 1969. In the centre background is the winder house and on the right the headgear. The conveyor from the crusher station feeds the ore bin. Note that there is a cross belt to dispose of waste in the foreground. The figure is the late J.H. Trounson.

Wheal Pendarves, Simms Shaft, 1968. An aerial view of the site during sinking operations.

Wheal Pendarves, Simms Shaft, 1969. Taken at the time the sinking of the shaft had just been completed.

Wheal Pendarves, 1970s. In connection with the operations at the new Simms Shaft certain other works had to be undertaken at old mine workings in the vicinity. This print shows Bennetts Shaft on Tryphena Mine. The headgear had been at West Wheal Peevor when the Barcas Mining Co. was working there.

Four
Chacewater to the Atlantic Coast

North Wheal Busy, Engine Shaft, early twentieth century. This was situated near the crossroads in the village of Blackwater. The engine house once contained a 45in pumping engine. In the background is one of three signal boxes at the Blackwater junction of the Great Western Railway and the embankment of the then new Chacewater-Newquay branch line.

Great Wheal Busy. The bob of the 85in Cornish pumping engine has been off-loaded from a railway waggon at Truro Station. This engine was built in Cornwall in 1852 by the Perran Foundry Co. for a mine at St Austell. It was later sold to Pencoed Colliery in South Wales and returned to Cornwall in 1909.

Great Wheal Busy, 1909. The bob of the large pumping engine being hauled by two traction engines from Truro to Chacewater when the mine was being re-opened.

Great Wheal Busy, c.1909. The new twenty-five head Californian Mill is being erected. The two locomotive-type boilers, which provided steam for the mill engine, are on the right.

Great Wheal Busy, c.1910. The building of the arsenic stack is nearly completed. Note that the long flue from the stack to the arsenic calciner is being built. The mill building occupies the centre of the photograph.

Great Wheal Busy, Harvey's Engine Shaft. The 85in engine photographed shortly after it had commenced work in about 1910.

Great Wheal Busy. The winding engine when being installed in the early years of the twentieth century.

Great Wheal Busy, c.1909. The small steam winding engine during erection, showing the drivers' control position.

Great Wheal Busy, c.1909. The mill engine.

Great Wheal Busy, c.1909. A view inside the mill dressing floors.

Great Wheal Busy, c.1910. The arsenic mill showing a typical arsenic barrel in which this dangerous substance was shipped.

Great Wheal Busy, c.1923. A hoisting shaft at the time of high arsenic prices.

Great Wheal Busy. Photographed in the late 1920s after the mine had closed and when the pitwork was being stripped out of Harvey's Shaft to the deep adit level. What appears to be a little hut on the left of the photograph is actually a former Redruth Brewery five ton Foden Steam Waggon. This had been taken out of retirement, jacked up off the ground and a winding drum built around the rear axle. From this improvised hoist a rope was carried to the nose of the beam of the engine and then down the shaft. Although this was a very dangerous method of working they succeeded in recovering a lot of scrap metal without incident!

Killifreth Mine, early 1890s. Left to right: Hawke's Shaft 80in pumping engine, the winding engine for Hawke's Shaft which also appears to have hoisted from Old Engine Shaft on the right.

Killifreth Mine. On the extreme left hand edge of the picture is Engine Shaft, after which is the beam winding engine house and Hawke's Shaft. On the skyline, right, is Black Dog Shaft engine house of Great Wheal Busy and in the foreground the Great Wheal Busy Mill. Photographed within the first decade of the twentieth century.

Killifreth Mine, Hawke's Shaft. This shows the gearwork of the 85in pumping engine which was the last engine to work at the mine. The machinery remained there for many years becoming progressively more derelict after the mine closed in the 1920s. This photograph was taken in the early 1920s when the engine was still at work.

Killifreth Mine, Hawke's Shaft, 1938, showing the main rod of the 85in pumping engine, the shaft pump column and the hotwell. In the background is the rotary winding engine house that hoisted at Hawke's Shaft. The figure is the late J.H. Trounson at that time aged thirty-three. He graduated from the Camborne School of Mines in 1926 and spent his professional career in Cornwall. During his lifetime he was a great champion of Cornish mining and became a noted mining historian.

Killifreth Mine, Hawke's Shaft, c.1935. Taken somewhat earlier than the previous photo. The boiler house is most unusual as it is constructed of weatherboarding with a corrugated iron roof. The steam pipe, which is not even lagged, is seen entering the engine house. On the left is the building that contained a large horizontal steam winding engine.

Portreath, early twentieth century, showing the inclined plane of the Portreath branch of the Hayle Railway. This was operated by a steam winding engine in the house at the top of the incline.

Portreath, 1923. A view of part of the harbour. At one time this busy port would have been full of vessels. They carried cargoes both incoming and outgoing – coal and other supplies inward, and ore from the mines outward. For a period in the nineteenth century, Portreath was served by a steam operated railway and a horse-drawn plateway, with each diverging to a different mining area. The railway link lasted until the 1930s.

Portreath. The great days of copper ore exports had ended by the time this photograph was taken in the late nineteenth century. However it remained a commercial port for a further fifty years or more. The principal commodity was coal from South Wales for the host of steam engines employed on the mines inland.

Portreath. A view of the harbour in the late nineteenth century showing three coasters tied up. Note the horse-drawn carts being loaded with coal on the left. The inclined plane bringing the railway to the harbour is in the middle ground of the photograph.

Wheal Noweth (the New Mine), *c.*1948. A tin prospect on the downs at Mingoose near St Agnes. This was commenced at the end of the Second World War by a former Wheal Kitty miner called Joe Yelland, aided by his son Martin. Other volunteers soon joined them. In this scene the late Donovan Wilkins is on the left operating the tackle (windlass). Joe Bendle is the "lander" awaiting the arrival of the kibble and Alan Thomas is pushing the tram to dump.

Wheal Noweth, Summer 1948. Martin Yelland at the shaft collar.

Wheal Noweth, c.1947. Another view of some of the young miners, showing Crispin Clemence, Joe Bendle and the author at the shaft collar. The light galvanised iron pipe appearing above the windlass ran to the bottom of the shaft and it will be noticed that it is curved at the top. After blasting this was turned into wind which blew the fumes up the shaft. This interesting little project came to an untimely halt when most of its "workforce" was mobilised for National Service.

West Wheal Towan. This mine was situated on the north coast between Portreath and Porthtowan. Here it is pictured in 1927 at the time Vivian's Shaft was being re-opened. The headgear is being erected and the tapered concrete chimney is virtually complete. A steam hoist and pumping plant were installed but no production ensued.

West Wheal Towan, Vivian's Shaft, c.1928. In this view all the plant is complete. Left to right: ore bin, headgear, pumping engine house, boiler house and winder house. In the background are the Blacksmith's shop, fitting shop etc.

West Wheal Towan, Vivian's Shaft, c.1928. The headgear and ore bin occupy the centre of the scene. On the right is the winding engine house with the steam pipe from the boiler house to supply the geared winder and capstan. The larger building on the left contained the horizontal single cylinder pumping engine built by Holman Brothers of Camborne. The engine previously worked at the North Dolcoath Mine near Camborne.

Wheal Sally, a small lead mine on the coast west of Porthtowan, in about 1922. After a certain amount of lead and zinc production, operations ceased around 1925.

Wheal Sally, c.1922. This view of the mine shows the stack of the vertical boiler smoking copiously. It provided steam for the winch and a diminutive Cornish pump.

Wheal Sally, a mine on the north coast between Portreath and Porthtowan, c.1924. At this time the company sank a new inclined shaft to a depth of about 260ft. This view shows the waste dump, headgear and winder house.

Wheal Lushington, Porthtowan, c.1910. The engine house was built in the 1880s to contain a rotary engine. This was to provide power to drive flat rods passing through a level (tunnel) in the hill behind. Where the level connected with a shaft, an angle bob was to be fixed, and by this means the mine was to be pumped out. The company promoting the venture was of doubtful financial standing and just after the engine parts were delivered to the site all operations ceased abruptly! The engine was scrapped but the house remains to this day and is currently a summer dwelling. Only a very small number of engine houses were built in Cornwall which did not have an engine erected.

Wheal Alfred, otherwise New Leisure, at Bolingey, Perranporth, shown early in the twentieth century at the commencement of operations.

Wheal Alfred, c.1909. This pictures the plant when it was in full operation and shows the winding engine house, headgear, capstan shears and other buildings connected with this little mine.

Wheal Alfred. A further view of the mine taken in 1909. The company installed an electricity generating plant powered by gas engines. The small Cornish pitwork was driven by an electric motor.

Penhale Mine, Perranporth. The beam winding engine is standing derelict on Penhale Point early in the twentieth century. The Count House may be seen to the left of the photo. The mine produced some copper, a little lead, over 7,000 ounces of silver and about 7,000 tons of iron ore.

Penhale Mine, early twentieth century. This engine house was originally built for an 80in Cornish pumping engine. In a later re-working of the mine a 66in engine was installed. In 1879 this engine was purchased by the Violet Seton Mine near Camborne and re-erected there. The beam winding engine in the background remained on site until scrapped many years later.

Penhale Mine. An early 1920s scene showing the count house on the left, the stack and house of the winding engine, together with the pumping engine house. All of these buildings were demolished in the Second World War following an enemy air attack on the nearby Penhale Military Camp in which a number of Army personnel were killed. The military authorities felt that these prominent buildings were a good landmark for aerial attack and ordered their destruction.

Penhale Mine in the early 1920s showing the pumping and winding engine houses of the mine at the eastern end of Perranporth beach. On the right hand edge of the scene is the engine house at Wheal Golden.

Tywarnhayle Mine, Porthtowan, Taylor's Engine Shaft, c.1907. This shows the electric sinking pump and motor in the attempted re-working of the mine at this time. The motor was rated at 100hp and the pump was capable of delivering 1,000 gallons per minute from the forty fathom level. The derelict Cornish pumping engine house is in the background.
Photograph: J.C. Burrow FRPS.

Tywarnhayle Mine, c.1908. An internal view of the electricity generating station, which used suction gas engines to drive the dynamos. This shows the electrical switch panel. Photograph: J.C. Burrow FRPS.

Tywarnhayle Mine, the generating station, c.1908. After mining operations ceased, this building was used by the Royal School of Mines until the late 1990s. They held a lease on the mine and maintained some of the underground workings above adit for the training of students – particularly in survey experience.
Photograph: J.C. Burrow FRPS.

Tywarnhayle Mine. An internal view of the small electric winder and capstan during the early twentieth century re-working.
Photograph: J.C. Burrow FRPS.

Tywarnhayle Mine, *c.*1910 A view of the generating station with exhaust rising from the gas engines. In the centre background is Taylor's Shaft and on the right Moncton's Shaft.